"FAITH FACTS"

A multifaith perspective

Jude Meryl

The Festival Shop Ltd.,
56 Poplar Road, Kings Heath, Birmingham, B14 7AG

© The Festival Shop Ltd. 1998

Note from the author : Working for seven years in the field of multifaith publications has given me an opportunity to meet people committed to bringing positivity to our understanding of the differences between faith communities, and to meet people who want basic information about multifaith issues, a topic which may be completely new to them. "Faith Facts" is a collation of information from a variety of sources, both written and experiential, which attempts to provide easily accessible, general information as a starting point for further exploration for those who are newly approaching the topic. To those working in the field of multifaith activities, many thanks are due from all of us for the often unsung but invaluable work they have already done, and continue to do, to alleviate tension and to promote understanding between the various faith communities that make up our multifaith country.

Published by The Festival Shop Ltd.

Cover Design by : Creative Touch Design
Printed by : Genesis Europrint, U.K.

ISBN 0 9535269 0 9

Contents

An Introduction to
"Faith Facts"

"Faith Facts" is a practical and easy to use guide for anyone needing basic information about some of the faith communities living in Britain today. This book includes sections on Buddhist, Christian, Hindu, Jewish, Muslim and Sikh faith communities.

"Faith Facts" looks at the topics of language, diet and dress. It looks, too, at visiting, both homes and places of worship, at everyday social occasions and at major life events such as births, marriages and funerals.

In consulting "Faith Facts", it cannot be stressed too highly that as members of faith communities and as individuals, we vary widely in our religious orthodoxy and with regard to the customs associated with our beliefs. Sometimes customs are more a matter of cultural tradition than they are of religious observance and because of this, presenting 'facts' is a challenging area and open to a large degree of interpretation. Nevertheless, some kind of practical guidelines are undoubtedly useful, and "Faith Facts" has therefore been written as an introduction for those who need basic information.

We offer "Faith Facts" in the spirit in which we anticipate it will be consulted - in the knowledge that there is always more to learn, and with respect.

Core belief

Buddhist belief entails taking advantage of being born as a human being to develop energetically the qualities of kindness and awareness in order to achieve freedom from suffering and to help others to do the same.

'Rules' of life

The Buddha taught that the way to enlightenment entails following an 'Eightfold Path', made up of right understanding, right thought, right speech, right action, right livelihood, right effort, right mindfulness, and right meditation. In practice, this might mean trying to live a life of positivity and care for others, refraining from causing injury to living creatures, and increasing personal awareness through the practice of meditation.

Important books

The 'Pali Canon' contains the teachings of the Buddha and his disciples, and is universally used by all schools of Buddhism. This is also known as the 'Three Baskets' and contains the three texts on Discipline, Discourses and Further Teachings.

The Mahayana school of Buddhists, in addition, refer specifically to 'sutras', or 'threads' of particular teaching themes, taken from the Discourses.

Both Theravada and Mahayana Buddhist schools popularly use the 'Jakata' stories, which are said to have been told by the Buddha, in teaching.

Daily acts of faith

A Buddhist would spend some time daily in meditation, and may also perform an act of devotion at a home shrine or Buddhist centre.

Major annual events

Varying Buddhist traditions commemorate different special events during the year, but those celebrated by all schools of Buddhism are :

Wesak - to remember Buddha's birth : a festival marked by the exchange of Wesak cards, perhaps depicting the Buddha or the lotus flower which is the symbol of purity and truth.

Full moon days - the Buddha is said to have been born at full moon : these are therefore days to remember especially the Buddha's teachings and to spend some time in meditation.

Births

The Buddha taught that being born as a human is a very unique opportunity to reach 'nirvana', the perfect state of being. The birth of a baby is, therefore, a time of special celebration for family and friends, and gifts for the baby, such as clothes, are generally very welcome.

As Buddhism is a way of life to be chosen, there are usually no specific religious ceremonies around the birth of a child, but babies born into a Buddhist household may be taken to a Buddhist temple to be blessed by the monks.

Names

It is usual for many Buddhists to have two or more names, the first of which may be the family name and the second or subsequent name/s the given name/s.

Where names are required for records, it is therefore advisable to ask first for the family name and to use this as the surname.

Diet

General : Buddhists are usually vegetarian, as butchery would be seen as 'intentional killing', a contravention of the teaching of the Buddha. Those Buddhists who are not fully vegetarian may eat fish or eggs. Strictly vegetarian Buddhists would not eat meat of any kind, nor anything that is produced from animals (such as cheese made with rennet). Many may also prefer to refrain from onions and from garlic.

Salt-free salads, rice, vegetables and fruit are generally acceptable foods to offer.

Specific : Full moon days and new moon days are often fast days for many Buddhists, as are some festival days for various schools of Buddhism. On days of fasting, a Buddhist may eat before noon, but not afterwards.

Language

Members of Buddhist families in the UK may speak several languages other than English, including Tibetan, Cantonese, Hakka, Japanese and Sinhalese.

Buddhist texts make use of two further languages. The 'Pali Canon' is written in Pali, a language derived from Sanskrit and believed to be the language closest to that spoken by the Buddha. In addition, many Buddhist texts from the Mahayana school of Buddhism are written in Sanskrit itself, an ancient sacred language not in use for contemporary, conversational purposes.

Dress

To check dress requirements for particular occasions, see the appropriate entry e.g. Marriages.

In general, there are no religious requirements for forms of everyday dress for lay Buddhists. Buddhist monks or nuns of the Theravada school shave their heads and wear orange or ochre coloured robes.

Visits

Places of worship : A Buddhist centre (or 'vihara') will usually contain a statue of the Buddha, a place for teaching and meditation and, sometimes, accommodation for monks or nuns. The focal point for worship is the shrine room, which generally contains a statue of the Buddha, together with incense, flowers and candles. Offerings of food, flowers and incense are customarily taken to the shrine room, and whilst visitors are not expected to make offerings, these will be welcome if proferred.

It is preferable that those entering the shrine room are dressed modestly and shoes should be removed before entering, as a sign of respect. Seating is usually on the floor, and quietness is appropriate, once inside. The shrine room is used for meditation, for teaching and for devotion ('puja'). Visitors are not expected to join in, but may do so if they wish.

Home visiting: Most Buddhists will have a shrine in the home, which may contain an image of the Buddha. This is the place where personal devotion is expressed through the offering of incense, flowers and candlelight. A gift of flowers would be acceptable when visiting.

Preparation before mealtimes customarily entails washing the hands, and the meal itself would generally be shared with thankfulness for the food offered and in a spirit of awareness of what is being eaten.

Marriages

A Buddhist wedding is not a sacred ceremony, but comprises the making of promises between the couple, in the style appropriate to their traditional or chosen culture. The marriage itself can be celebrated in any suitable place, often the bride's home. Dress etiquette would dictate the wearing of 'best clothes', in whichever way this most discreetly, modestly and unobtrusively reflects the guest's own tradition.

Wedding cards are generally welcome but, in choosing a card, it would be appropriate to remember that many Buddhist weddings are 'arranged' so that close members of the family have been involved in the choice of a life partner for bride and groom. Ideas for wedding presents may include gifts such as red candles, candleholders , incense and decorative incense burners, flowers and vases, or statues of the Buddha.

The wedding may be presided over by any suitable adult, often the bride's uncle or cousin. The couple promise to be considerate to each other, to love and to have respect for one another.

After the wedding, there may be a visit to the local vihara in order to have the marriage blessed by monks. If this is the case, the families of the couple may also renew their promises to keep the five Precepts which form the basic 'rules' of lay Buddhism and which form the foundation of 'Right Action'.

After the wedding ceremonies, there is generally feasting for the bride and groom, relatives and guests, before the couple begin their new life together.

Funerals

Acceptance of death is a key Buddhist philosophy, as death brings with it the hope that the deceased may this time escape rebirth and attain 'nirvana', the perfect state of being.

If the deceased was a member of a traditional Buddhist background, mourners at the funeral may dress in white, otherwise modest dress in neutral colours would be appropriate. Buddhists are generally cremated, usually three to seven days after death. Traditional Buddhist funerals can be quite elaborate. The Three Jewels (reminders to all Buddhists of the things they can trust in - the Buddha, his teaching and his followers), and the Five Precepts (guidelines for living a good life) may be recited at the vihara as a way of reminding the mourners about how best to live the rest of their lives. The cremation may be followed by music and a feast to celebrate the life of the deceased. Other Buddhist funerals may be quieter, with a memorial eulogy being accepted practice, together with readings from specially chosen Buddhist texts.

Medical Matters

Family planning : Some Buddhists might consider contraception to be an interference ; the decision is usually left to the couple concerned.

Illness : Many Buddhists may traditionally and culturally favour the use of home remedies in the case of illness, with rice gruel (one part rice to two parts water) often being seen as particularly beneficial for successful convalescence.

Hospital stays : In medical circumstances, a Buddhist monk or nun would prefer to be treated by a member of staff of the same sex. In cases of a longer hospital stay, showers are considered to be preferable to baths, and a container of water for washing purposes should be provided whenever the toilet area is separate from a bathroom. There are no religious objections to blood transfusion, or transplants, other than the stipulation that life should not be destroyed in the pursuit of these.

If a patient is terminally ill, it is important to remember that many Buddhists will wish to maintain a clear mind when dying. This may entail the refusal of pain relieving drugs, if these would impair mental alertness.

In the case of death : After death, the body of the deceased may be handled by non-Buddhists, but a monk from the same school of Buddhism as the deceased should be informed promptly, in order that prayers may be recited as soon as possible after the death. There are no religious objections to autopsies.

Core belief

Christians believe in living according to the loving nature of God as revealed by Jesus' life and death, helped in this task by the Holy Spirit and by communicating with God through prayer.

'Rules' of life

All Christians would try to follow the example that Jesus taught and lived, one of the foremost tenets of which is to 'love one's neighbour as oneself'. Many Christians would believe also in trying to keep the Judaic Ten Commandments. In practice, this might mean trying to meet everyday situations with a 'Christlike' response, arrived at through prayer, quiet reflection and consultation of the Scriptures.

Holy books

The Christian scriptures are called 'The Bible', which comprises both 'New' and 'Old' Testaments.

The 'Old Testament' contains the books of the Hebrew scriptures, to which Jesus testified, and which Christians therefore consider to be part also of the Christian body of scriptures. The 'New Testament' includes four accounts of the life of Jesus (the 'Gospels'), a series of accounts of the early churches ('The Acts' and 'The Epistles') and other writings such as the 'Book of Revelation'.

In addition to this, the writings of the early church 'Fathers' and various Christian saints play an important part in Christian teachings.

Daily acts of faith

Many Christians pray daily, particularly before sleep, and often use 'The Lord's Prayer' which Jesus taught his disciples. Collective worship on a Sunday is usual.

The regular sharing of bread and wine is important for many Christians, but the frequency of this act of remembrance varies according to the Christian tradition followed. In addition, many Christians follow an individual programme of devotion that may include studying the Scriptures, private prayer and meditation.

Major annual events

The most widely celebrated Christian festivals are :

Christmas - to celebrate Christ's birth : a joyous festival marked by the exchange of cards and presents.

Lent - to commemorate Christ's sojourn in the wilderness : a time of fasting and penitence.

Easter - in commemoration of Christ's death and resurrection : a joyous festival marked by the exchange of cards depicting light, flowers or the cross.

Ascension Day - to commemorate the day on which Christ finally ascended into the heavens : a day of quiet remembrance, always taking place on a Thursday.

Pentecost / Whitsun - to celebrate the coming of the Holy Spirit to Christ's disciples : a day characterised by the colour white, often in the form of a white dove, symbol of the Holy Spirit at Christ's baptism.

Births

Jesus taught that children are to be made welcome, and the birth of a baby in a Christian household is a cause for celebration. Cards of congratulations for the family of the child, and gifts of flowers, or clothes for the baby are usually very much appreciated at this time.

For many Christian sects, it is important for a baby to be 'baptised' or 'christened' (the ritual washing away of original sin by water) when an infant. This ceremony is a joyful opportunity for friends and family to welcome the new baby into the family of the church, 'godfathers' and 'godmothers' are chosen and the baby is given its 'Christian' names.

Names

Most Christians have at least two names : one or more 'Christian' names, followed by a family name which for men remains constant, but may change for women if they follow the custom of adopting their husband's family name once they are married.

Where names are required for records, it is advisable to ask first for the 'surname' and then for the other name/s.

Diet

General : Although some Christian sects ban the use of stimulating substances (such as alcohol, tobacco, tea and coffee) and encourage vegetarianism, Christians in general are not religiously forbidden to eat any particular kinds of foods.

Specific : Most Christians would traditionally undertake some kind of fast or abstinence as a spiritual discipline during the period of Lent. Fasting at other times of the year can be a preparation for communion, an act of penitence, or an individual act of devotion.

Language

As Christianity is ethnically diverse, members of Christian families in the UK may speak several languages other than English, depending on their cultural background.

Church services would generally take place in the language of the host country, although in some churches Latin is used, whilst other English churches may use seventeenth century English, rather than modern day English for particular services. 'The Bible', although written originally in Hebrew and ancient Greek, is generally read in translation.

Dress

To check dress requirements for particular occasions, see the appropriate entry e.g. Marriages.

Although some Christian sects may issue their own guidelines, in general Christians are not enjoined in matters of everyday wear to dress in a particular way.

Religious orders of Christian monks and nuns may have forms of dress which would generally entail the wearing of darker colours, full length robes and head coverings for women.

Visits

Places of worship : A Christian place of worship may vary greatly in its presentation, from a plain room to an ornate and richly decorated building. It would be usual, however, to find a focal point, (from flowers and the Bible on a table, to a draped altar) and to find seats of some kind for the congregation to use. Offerings of money are customarily taken to a Christian place of worship, to be made either during or after the service, and whilst visitors are not expected to make offerings, these will be welcome if proferred.

Dress etiquette varies, but visitors would generally find it acceptable to be dressed modestly. It is traditional in most Christian places of worship for men to bare their heads before entering, and in some places for a woman to cover her head.

Inside the building, seating is on chairs or rows of benches ('pews'). During the service, worshippers may stand, sit and kneel at various points, and visitors are welcome to follow the same procedures, remaining seated if kneeling does not seem appropriate. Visitors are welcome to join in with prayers and hymns, but if the service involves taking bread and wine, visitors are not generally expected to partake - either pass the plate and cup to the person sitting next to you, or remain seated whilst other worshippers move to the front of the church. Neither are visitors expected to make the sign of the cross or kneel to the altar as worshippers may do during the course of some church services.

Home visiting : Some Christians may have a small shrine at home, with sacred pictures, flowers and a candle. A copy of the Bible would normally be kept in a Christian household, and the wearing of a cross as a pendant is common. A gift of flowers for the host/ess is generally acceptable.

Christians prefer to wash their hands before eating, and to bless their food before beginning, with a short prayer or 'grace'. Visitors may wish to follow the lead of their hosts by sitting, or standing quietly, whilst this takes place.

Marriages

For Christians, marriage is a ceremony which takes place 'in the presence of God', in front of a priest and before witnesses, and the couple make vows which join them in a partnership for life. The marriage is celebrated in a Christian place of worship, and it is therefore advisable for wedding guests to wear 'best clothes' of a colourful but modest nature. The bride traditionally marries in white or ivory colours.

Sending wedding congratulations cards to the bride and groom is usual, as is the giving of wedding presents which will be useful for life in their new home together, such as linen, china or glassware. It is traditional at some weddings, to throw 'confetti' (small pieces of coloured paper shapes) over the couple as they leave the church.

After the couple have publicly made their vows to love and care for each other and any children they may have, it is traditional for the bride and groom to exchange rings to show that they are now married, and to sign the register before leaving the place of worship.

The wedding is generally followed by feasting for the bride and groom, relatives and guests before the bride changes her clothes and she and the groom leave for their holiday alone together, called their 'honeymoon', as the start to their new married life.

Funerals

Christian teaching is that death is not to be feared as, following Jesus' own death, he lived again and gave those who have faith, the promise of eternal life. For Christians, therefore, death is a beginning rather than an ending, although expressions of sympathy and support for the loss of the family of the deceased are appropriate, often in the form of a card or letter of condolence.

Mourners at a Christian funeral usually dress in black, and it is traditional for those who knew the deceased to attend the funeral in order to pay their last respects, even if not specifically invited.

Christians may be either buried or cremated. Often, there is a service first at the place of worship previously attended by the deceased, where it is customary for the person leading the service to speak about the life of the deceased. This is followed by a procession to the graveyard or crematorium, where a much shorter service takes place for the committal of the body.

A simple meal for invited friends and family at the family home usually follows the committal.

Medical Matters

Family planning : Many Christian sects believe that family planning is a matter of individual responsibility, although churches may vary on whether or not the choice of contraceptive method is a matter for religious guidance.

Illness : Christian teaching advocates both visiting the sick and praying for their return to health. Visits from friends and relatives, or cards and flowers from well-wishers are therefore welcome in times of illness.

Hospital stays : In cases of a longer hospital stay, there are several sacraments available to Christians who are ill. For some traditions, confession of sins acts as a spiritual cleansing, an ill person may be anointed, or prayers may be said with laying on of hands. Bread and wine can also be brought to those who are too ill to reach a place of worship. It should be remembered that privacy is essential for the carrying out of any of these sacraments. Blood transfusions and transplants are not forbidden on religious grounds, except by Jehovah's Witnesses.

If a patient is terminally ill, they may wish to keep a copy of the Bible at hand, and the prayers and presence of friends, relatives and clergy are much appreciated.

In the case of death : After death, the body of the deceased may be handled by non-Christians, but should be treated with as much respect as if it were still alive. There are no religious objections to autopsies.

Core belief

To learn how to be reunited with God - of whom all living beings are eternally part - and to learn this through study, devotion, prayer and service to others.

'Rules' of life

One of the Hindu sacred texts, 'The Bhagavad-Gita', suggests 'Three Pathways' which are : to cultivate knowledge by studying the ancient texts (the 'Way of Knowledge') ; to practise exercises for the mind and body which help towards a deeper and better state of meditation (the 'Way of Action') ; and to maintain devotion by developing and expressing love for God through prayer and service (the 'Way of Devotion').

In practice, most Hindus would believe in the sanctity of life, adopt vegetarianism, and support the concept of tolerance towards those of other races and religions.

Holy books

The Hindu ancient scriptures are called 'The Vedas', and contain, amongst other texts 'The Upanishads' (philosophical works discussing the purpose of life) and 'The Brahmanas' (advice on ritual).

The popular Hindu epics deal mainly with questions of morality and are 'The Ramayana' and 'The Mahabharata'(from which 'The Bhagavad-Gita' is taken).

In popular use, in addition to these, are the 'Laws of Manu' (ancient texts containing guidance on social practice), and the 'Puranas' (stories about the exploits of the incarnations of the Hindu deities).

Daily acts of faith

Hindus would generally perform a daily act of personal devotion at home, either alone or with others.

Major annual events

Amongst the most widely celebrated Hindu festivals are :

Holi - to celebrate the death of winter : a joyous festival marked with the throwing of coloured dyes.

Rama Navami - to celebrate the birth of Rama, seventh incarnation of the deity, Vishnu : at which festival the epic of Rama, 'The Ramayana', is often recited.

Janamashtami - to celebrate the birth of Krishna, eighth incarnation of the deity, Vishnu : at which festival there is fasting until midnight, when a symbolic image of Krishna is welcomed into the temple with flowers and great rejoicing.

Divali - to honour the deity, Lakshmi, and celebrate the symbolic reunion of Rama and his wife, Sita : at which festival Divali lamps and candles are lit to fill homes with light, and Divali cards are exchanged to wish people a 'Happy Divali'.

Shivaratri - in honour of the deity, Shiva : a night spent in prayer, fasting and meditation.

Births

The birth of a baby is always a cause for celebration, with the arrival of the first boy being especially welcome in many households. Gifts of clothes for the new baby are generally very acceptable. Mothers are traditionally expected to rest for forty days after the birth, in order to avoid chills and other debilitating illnesses.

Babies' names are not always made known straight away. As soon as possible after the birth, prayers are whispered in the child's ear, honey is put on the tongue and the baby is given a name which is kept secret until later.

Names

Members of Hindu families may have three or four names, depending upon cultural background and tradition. It is quite usual to have : a given, or personal name, complimentary name/s (a father's given name or the name of a deity, for example) and a family name (which may or may not indicate social grouping).

Where names are required for records, it is advisable to use the individual's last name, in every case, as a surname.

Diet

General : Hindus in general do not eat beef. Orthodox Hindus are strictly vegetarian, eating no meat, no eggs and nothing that is produced from animals (such as cheese made with rennet). Many may prefer also to refrain from alcohol, from onions and from garlic.

Salt-free salads, rice, vegetables and fruit are generally acceptable foods to offer, and a less strict diet would allow cottage cheese, yoghurt and milk as part of a menu.

Specific : Festivals which may require fasting are : Janamashtami (a celebration to commemorate Krishna's birth) and Shivaratri (in honour of the deity, Shiva).

Language

Members of Hindu families in the UK may speak several languages other than English, including Gujarati, Hindi, Punjabi and Bengali.

The language in which the major Hindu sacred texts are written is Sanskrit, which is not in use as a contemporary, conversational language.

Dress

To check dress requirements for particular occasions, see the appropriate entry e.g. Marriages.

In general, it is not considered acceptable for a Hindu girl or woman to have uncovered legs. The wearing of a 'sari' is traditional, or a top over loose trousers for everyday wear for younger girls. Covering the body is generally a requirement and so tact in discussing joining in with activities such as swimming, and in providing individual changing areas for sports would therefore be appreciated.

Visits

Places of worship : Although collective worship does take place at the home shrine, the 'mandir'(temple), is the place at which most festivals are celebrated and teaching takes place.

Inside the mandir is the shrine where the 'murtis' (representations of the deities) stand. There may also be a decorated seat for the 'swami', who may lead the worship.

Offerings of food or money are customarily taken to the mandir to be presented on arrival and, whilst visitors are not expected to make offerings, these will be welcome if proferred, remembering that food should not be cooked.

Visitors are expected to dress modestly, with a head covering for women needed. Seating is on the floor, sometimes with men and boys on one side and women and girls on the other. It is usual to sit during the ceremony, with legs crossed or to the side : it is considered disrespectful to sit with feet pointing towards the sacred area at the front of the temple. Sometimes standing is appropriate during the 'arti'(ceremony).

After food has been blessed during the ceremony, it is distributed, and visitors will be expected to partake, accepting the food in cupped hands, with the right hand uppermost.

Home visiting : A Hindu home will usually have a household shrine. This is the place where 'puja' (worship) is performed, often at dusk, with prayers, bells and incense.

Preparation before mealtimes entails washing the hands. At the meal itself, the food is often blessed by offering it to the deities and sprinkling it with water, some food is often put aside for the arrival of the unexpected guest as no one should be turned away hungry from the door, and a little may be set apart to be given to animals or birds. During the meal it is polite to take food and eat it with the right hand only and after the meal it is customary to give thanks and to wash the hands. Culturally, the offering of hospitality is seen as a sacred duty, so being a considerate guest in a Hindu household involves a willingness to reciprocate by sharing in the food and drink offered.

Marriages

A Hindu marriage can be celebrated in any suitable place, such as a house, a hall or in the open air, the actual wedding ceremony taking place under a specially constructed canopy. In general, it is advisable to follow dress etiquette as for a visit to a place of worship, but, in addition, to know that red or deep pink are considered to be auspicious colours to wear at a wedding celebration. The bride herself will usually marry in red or deep pink fabrics, decorated with gold thread, whilst the groom is given garlands to wear on his arrival.

Wedding cards are generally welcome but, in choosing a card, it would be appropriate to remember that many Hindu weddings are 'arranged', so that close members of the family are involved in the choice of a life partner for bride and groom. Ideas for wedding presents may include decorative gifts, such as jewellery for the bride, or ornaments for the home, wrapped in red or gold. It is also a good idea to take some rice grains to the wedding, as these are traditionally thrown over the bride with the hope that she will have many children.

The marriage couple make their vows at a ceremony presided over by a priest, and known as 'The Seven Steps'. They walk around a sacred fire (symbol of the presence of God), their steps symbolic of their future walk together and their commitment to carrying out seven duties which include supporting one another, earning a living to provide a home for each other and any children they may have, and working to become lifelong friends as well as marriage partners. After the marriage, the bride may have a red spot painted on her forehead, or have her hairline decorated in red by the groom as a sign of her new status.

After the wedding ceremonies there is generally feasting for the bride and groom, relatives and guests, at the end of which the bride changes into new clothes and leaves, to begin living with her husband and his family.

Funerals

As a response to death, a trait of Hinduism is to encourage a state of philosophical acceptance of it, Hindu belief being that the soul of the deceased will either be reborn or has completed the cycle of rebirth and can rejoin the Creator.

Those attending the funeral dress in white as the colour of mourning and Hindus are, generally, cremated (although children under five may be buried). It is traditional for the eldest son of the deceased to take a leading part in the after-death ceremonies, however young he may be, including consigning the body to the flames at the crematorium.

Family and friends may join the family of the deceased at the cremation, and also on the fourth and eleventh day after the death has occurred, to share with the family in their offerings of rice and milk for the deceased at the family shrine. Sometimes, the ashes of the deceased are sent to family members in India, for scattering on the sacred River Ganges. Traditionally, ten or twelve days are observed as the mourning period.

Medical Matters

Family planning : Hinduism places no restriction on the use of contraception.

Illness : The ancient practice of Ayurvedic medicine (with advice, for example, on diet, sleep, hygiene, clothing and exercise) is still followed today by many Hindus. This may mean that certain foods are unacceptable during illness : milk and citrus fruit, for example, when suffering from a cough. In general, home remedies are favoured in the first instance.

Hospital stays : In medical circumstances, most Hindu women would indicate a preference to be treated or examined by a female doctor or nurse, and would not wish to be sent for relevant tests in a short gown. In cases of a longer hospital stay, showers are considered to be preferable to baths, and a container of water for washing purposes should always be provided whenever the toilet area is separate from a bathroom. There are no religious objections to organ donation and transplants.

If a patient is terminally ill, preparation for the dying person may entail hearing readings from the Hindu scriptures, having a thread tied around neck or wrist, being sprinkled with water from the sacred River Ganges, or having relatives bring money or clothing to be touched before they are distributed to the needy.

In the case of death : After death, the body must be kept covered and it is preferable for the family to handle the body, the eldest son or other senior male relative being consulted in all arrangements. There are no religious objections to autopsies.

Core belief

Jews wish to live according to God's laws, as revealed by Moses, the most important of which is to believe in one God and to learn to love God through study, through prayer and by celebrating the yearly cycle of holy days.

'Rules' of life

Jews believe that God's will was made manifest through the revelation given to Moses, the 'Torah', which includes the 'commandments' (or laws) that relate to every aspect of life, both spiritual and social. The interpretation of these laws is therefore a focus for personal and communal life. In practice, this would mean believing in one God, keeping the Ten Commandments and bringing the qualities of compassion and justice into everyday life.

Holy books

The Jewish scriptures are known as the 'Tanakh' and include the 'Torah' (the five books of Moses), the 'Nevi'im' (including the books of the Prophets, Judges and Kings) and the 'Ketuvim' ('Writings' which include the Books of Esther and Ruth).

In addition to the scriptures, other popularly consulted Jewish writings are the 'Talmud', which relates in more detail to ritual, law and ethical guidance, and the 'Midrash' which comprises parables, legends and stories from the early 'rabbis' (teachers).

Daily acts of faith

All practising Jews recite a daily prayer called the 'Shema' ('Hear') which is a fundamental affirmation of faith. Sabbath, from sunset on Friday evening until sunset on Saturday evening, is generally observed by Jews as a day of rest. Attendance at synagogue, saying of prayers and a family meal also form part of the observance, although strictness of observance depends upon degree of orthodoxy.

Major annual events

The observance of festivals is of great importance in Jewish life, and falls into several categories :

The *'Days of Awe'* - including **Rosh Hashanah**, the New Year and a time of penitence and **Yom Kippur**, a day of fasting.

The *'Three Foot Festivals'* - three festivals when, traditionally, all Jews went to Jerusalem. These are : **Sukkot** which commemorates the wanderings of the children of Israel, **Pesach** which commemorates the Exodus from Egypt and **Shavuot** which commemorates the receiving of the 'Torah'.

The *minor festivals* which include the popular festivals of **Chanukah** - a festival of light, **Purim** - a reminder of the story of Esther and **Tishah B'Av** - to commemorate the historical destruction of the Temple.

Births

As each newly-born life is seen as being a unique gift from God, and Judaism is intrinsically a family-centred faith, the birth of a baby is a very happy occasion and gifts such as clothing for the baby are generally welcome.

About eight days after the birth of a male child, his Brit Milah (ritual circumcision and naming) takes place, usually at home, followed by a family party. The name of a girl child is given by her father before the whole congregation when he is called to the platform at the synagogue on the Sabbath following her birth.

Names

It is usual for Jewish children to have one or more given names, often taken from Biblical sources, followed by a family name.

Where names are required for records, it is advisable to ask first for the 'surname' and then for the other names.

Diet

General : Jews are religiously required to uphold the 'Kashrut', a series of special dietary laws which refer to the provision of 'kosher' food (food prepared in a specially prescribed way). In general, Jews do not eat pork in any form, and would not wish to eat meat and milk products at the same meal. 'Kosher' foods may be obtained from specialised food shops, but the provision of a vegetarian meal would probably be more acceptable, as this would not bring into doubt the utensils used for preparation. Presenting a variety of plain salad, vegetable and fruit dishes may be generally advisable, with dairy-free dressings or sauces to hand if required.

Specific : Minor fast days may be observed throughout the year, but 'Yom Kippur'(The Day of Atonement) is a major annual, twenty-five hour fast observed by the majority of Jews. In addition to this, no leavened bread is eaten during the period of Passover when unleavened bread called 'matzah' may be obtained instead.

Language

Members of Jewish families in the UK would generally use English as their main language of communication, although Hebrew or Yiddish are conversationally spoken in some Jewish households.

The Jewish scriptures are written in Hebrew, and this is also the main language of worship, learned by many children in synagogue class. Prayer books in the synagogue therefore open from right to left since Hebrew is written in this way.

Dress

To check dress requirements for particular occasions, see the appropriate entry e.g. Marriages.

Everyday dress requirements differ with degree of orthodoxy. For Orthodox women and girls it is necessary to keep the body and limbs covered, and in some cases also the hair. Tact in discussing joining in with activities such as swimming would be appreciated.

Visits

Places of worship : Inside the synagogue there is often a raised platform from which the 'Torah' is read. The handwritten 'Torah' scroll itself is in a covered alcove before which a lamp is kept alight to remind worshippers of the constant presence of God.

A box called a 'mezuzah', on the internal doors of the synagogue contains a piece of parchment scroll on which is written the first parts of the 'Shema' (the daily prayer). Visitors are asked to avoid taking non-kosher food into the synagogue itself.

It is preferable for visitors to be dressed modestly, with arms and legs covered, and women wearing a knee length skirt or dress, rather than trousers. In Orthodox synagogues, women cover their heads ; men and boys should cover their heads when visiting all synagogues. In some synagogues, women and men sit separately and sometimes there is a special balcony area for women to sit in. Visitors are not expected to join in with worship, but are welcome to do so if they wish. After the service, 'kiddush' (sanctification by blessings) may be said over bread and wine and this is then shared. Visitors are welcome to share this bread and wine if they wish.

Home Visiting : In most Jewish households, a 'mezuzah' is positioned on the right hand doorpost of each room except the bathroom and toilet, as a symbol of the sanctity of the home. A gift of flowers would be acceptable when visiting.

Religious preparation before mealtimes entails washing the hands, and the meal is preceded by the saying of one blessing or more, depending on the type of meal to be eaten. Visitors may wish to follow the lead of their hosts by attending quietly whilst this takes place.

Marriages

For Jewish couples, the wedding is a spiritual and a practical celebration of their intention to share their lives with each other. A Jewish wedding takes place in a synagogue, conducted by the rabbi, and it is therefore advisable for wedding guests to bear in mind the guidelines for dress when visiting a synagogue. The bride herself traditionally marries in white or ivory colours.

Wedding cards are generally welcome, with perhaps an image of a wine glass, 'menorah' (seven branched candlestick) or a gold ring. Ideas for wedding gifts may include items which would be useful for the couple's new home together, such as china or glassware.

The marriage ceremony itself takes place under a canopy inside the synagogue. The couple read and sign their written marriage contract and share wine from the same glass, which is then ritually broken under the groom's foot at the end of the ceremony, and it is traditional for the bride to receive a wedding ring. When the couple step out from under the canopy, it is customary for the guests to call out 'Mazel Tov' ('Good luck and be happy').

After the wedding, there is feasting, music and dancing for bride and groom and family and friends before the couple leave to begin their new life together.

Funerals

Jewish belief is that, after death, the deceased has gone to be with God, who will fairly judge the life the deceased has led. Funerals generally take place as soon as possible, usually within twenty-four hours.

Orthodox Jews are always buried, in special Jewish burial grounds. Burial is preferred for most Jews, although some liberal Jews may choose cremation. A service is held at the burial ground, which it is appropriate for family, friends and colleagues to attend, dressed as for a visit to a synagogue. Prayers are said for the deceased, and it is customary for the family to assist with the burial of the coffin. Funerals are plain, and donations of flowers, for example, are not appropriate.

Following the funeral, there is a mourning period of seven days for the family of the deceased, during which collective prayers are said and mourners may visit the bereaved with condolences and gifts of food. During this time, members of the family are not expected to return to work.

Medical Matters

Family planning : Many Jews would believe that family planning is a matter of individual responsibility although some would consider it a matter for religious guidance.

Illness : As Judaism to a large extent encourages an awareness of diet and everyday health care, Jews are generally questioning patients who are inclined to refer to professional health carers in cases of illness. Visiting the sick is a solemn duty for members of the Jewish faith, with prayer forming an important part of their support.

Hospital stays : In medical situations, an Orthodox Jewess would prefer to be treated by a member of staff of the same sex. Blood transfusions are subject to personal decision-making. Transplants and organ donations, however, are generally a matter for religious guidance.

If a patient is terminally ill, it is important to remember that it is a basic tenet of Judaism that a dying person should not be left alone, and that the presence of a companion who will read to or say prayers with the patient would be usual.

In the case of death : The 'Chevra Kadisha' (Holy Brotherhood) should be notified immediately after the death, and they will then take charge of all arrangements for the burial procedures, but will not move the body on the Sabbath. Autopsies, unless ordered by civil authorities, are forbidden in Jewish law.

Core belief

To submit life to the will of Allah as revealed by the Prophet Muhammad through the 'Qur'an' and to do so through a declaration of faith, regular prayer, almsgiving, fasting and pilgrimage.

'Rules' of life

The essentials of the Muslim faith are encapsulated in what are known as the 'Five Pillars of Islam'. These form the basis of conduct for all practising Muslims and consist of a *Declaration of Faith* in Allah and in Muhammad as his messenger, ritual *Prayer* five times a day, *Almsgiving* for the service of the needy, annual *Fasting* during the month of Ramadan between dawn and sunset as a spiritual discipline, and *Pilgrimage* to Makkah at least once in a lifetime.

Holy book

The holy book for all Muslims is the 'Qu'ran', which is believed to have been given directly by Allah to the Prophet Muhammad by revelation, and is used as a source of guidance for all aspects of life.

Reference is also made, however, to the 'Hadith', which are generally recognised collections of material containing accounts of the words and actions of the Prophet Muhammad during his lifetime.

Daily acts of faith

Daily prayer is religiously prescribed, and should take place at around dawn, midday, late afternoon, after sunset and late evening. As daily prayer is obligatory for Muslims, tactful discussion concerning the provision of suitable washing facilities for pre-prayer ablutions, and the privacy and time to conduct prayers would be appreciated in workplace or place of education.

Major annual events

The First of Muharram - which begins the Islamic New Year : a commemoration of the Prophet Muhammad's establishment of the Islamic social order.

Milad-un Nabi - to commemorate the Prophet Muhammad's birth : a day of prayer.

Lailat-ul Bara'at - when Allah is believed to determine the fate of humankind for the coming year : a time of fasting and all-night prayer.

Ramadan - the ninth month of the Muslim year : a time of fasting from sunrise to sunset each day as a spiritual discipline and time to deepen devotion.

Eid-ul Fitr - which ends the month of Ramadan when the new moon is sighted : a day of quiet celebration and an appropriate occasion on which to send 'Eid' cards or to wish friends a 'Happy Eid'.

Eid-ul Adha - which marks the end of the time of annual Pilgrimage : a day of thankfulness, marked by feasting and distribution of food to the needy.

Births

A child born into a Muslim family is seen as being a gift from Allah. Births are joyous occasions, and gifts of clothes or shawls for the baby are generally very welcome.

As soon as possible after the child's birth, a member of the family will recite a prayer quietly in the baby's ear, and a boy child will be circumcised as soon as this can be arranged. The new baby is named about seven days later at a ceremony called the 'Aqiqah', where his/her hair is shaved off to mark a new start in life, and there is a feast for family and friends, with a donation of food or money to the needy.

Names

It is usual for Muslims to have several personal or religious names, as many Muslims are named after the Prophet or someone in his family. The name of the family into which someone has been born is not necessarily used.

Where names are required for records, it is therefore advisable to ask first for the 'family' name and, if this is not available, to register the 'most used personal name' as a surname, followed by the lesser used names.

Diet

General : Muslims are religiously forbidden to eat pork or any pork by-product, nor should these items come into contact with any other food to be eaten. The consumption of alcohol is also totally forbidden. Muslims are allowed to eat poultry, mutton and beef, as long as the meat is 'halal' which means killed and prepared by a Muslim according to Islamic law.

A vegetarian meal would probably be most acceptable, perhaps 'falafel'(chickpea cakes with cayenne, cumin and coriander), remembering that the food should be well seasoned and spiced as bland foods are considered to be genuinely unpalatable.

Specific : Ramadan is a month of obligatory fasting for all Muslims between the hours of dawn and sunset. Young children are encouraged to do without snacks and sweets, as a preparation for missing full meals.

Language

Members of Muslim families in the UK may speak several languages other than English, including Urdu, Gujarati, Bengali, Punjabi, Turkish, Farsi and Hausa.

Because Arabic is the language in which the 'Qu'ran' was revealed by Allah to the Prophet Muhammad, Muslim children begin to learn it when they have reached the age of seven. Knowledge of Arabic is therefore widespread, both in order to read the 'Qu'ran' directly and because it is used as the main language of worship.

Dress

To check dress requirements for particular occasions, see the appropriate entry e.g. Marriages.

Degrees of modesty in dress differ, but it is customary for Muslim women to have at least a head covering, and often to be covered from head to foot when appearing in public places, and for men to be covered from waist to knee. Covering the body is generally a requirement : tact in discussing joining in with activities such as swimming, and in providing individual changing areas for sports would therefore be appreciated. It is worth noting that some devout male Muslims may prefer to keep their heads covered at all times.

Visits

Places of worship : Inside the 'mosque' the floor is generally carpeted and there is a raised pulpit from which the 'imam' teaches.

Visitors, both male and female are requested to wear modest clothing, ie ankle length skirts or trousers of a loose fitting kind. Women are also requested to wear long-sleeved and high necked tops, to cover the head with a scarf, and to avoid visiting a mosque when they are menstruating. Young children do not usually visit except for the Eid festivals. Shoes are always removed before entering the mosque.

Women and men enter by separate doors, and sit in separate parts of the mosque, once inside. Visitors may be greeted in Arabic ('Peace be upon you') and may respond ('Peace be upon you too') but it is not usual to shake hands with members of the opposite sex from oneself. Seating is on the floor, and care should be taken not to point the feet towards the 'Qibla' (the wall with a niche in it which shows the direction of Makkah). Visitors are welcome to sit quietly at a place near the back of the mosque whilst prayers are in progress, but are not expected to join in.

Home visiting : The free mixing of unrelated men and women is not customary in Islam, and this might be taken into account when visits are being arranged.

Muslim homes do not contain pictures of the Prophet Muhammad, but beautifully decorated pictures of religious buildings, or mosaic patterns are traditional. A gift of attractively decorated sweets might be offered to the hostess, once care has been taken that the sweets do not contain animal fat.

Preparation before mealtimes entails washing the hands, and prayers of thanks are said before the meal begins. After the meal, it is customary to wash the hands again.

Marriages

A Muslim marriage is seen as a human, not a sacred contract, but one based upon teachings from the 'Qu'ran' on how best to conduct family life. The wedding generally takes place at the bride's home and guests might wear 'best' clothes, bearing in mind that mixed company dictates modesty for men and women. The bride herself traditionally marries in red or deep pink.

Generally, wedding cards with decorative patterns may be acceptable, remembering when writing greetings that, in some cases, the wedding may have been 'arranged', so that close members of the family have been involved in the choice of an appropriate life partner for the bride and groom. Ideas for wedding presents may include decorative gifts for the home, such as cut glass, and it is usual for sweets (not containing animal fat) to be given during the ceremonies.

A contract is drawn up between the couple before the marriage. This is signed either before or on the same day as the wedding, which can be conducted by any adult Muslim male. During the wedding, which often takes place with the bride and groom in separate rooms, a witness from each of the families hears the promises and answers of the couple and transmits them to the other : the couple are asked three times whether they agree to the marriage. Following a recitation from the 'Qu'ran' the couple sign their contract, if they have not already done so, and there is feasting, customarily with women and men still separate, before the couple leave for the bridegroom's home.

Funerals

Muslim belief is that Allah chooses when a human being should be born and should die, and that, following death, each individual's unique life will be judged by Allah on the Day of Judgement. Formal and active mourning for a time immediately after the death is customary, requiring tact and understanding, but, longer term, a quiet acceptance of death as the will of Allah is philosophically very important for Muslims.

Funerals take place if at all possible within twenty-four hours of death, and are always burials. Modest dress in neutral colours, following guidelines for a visit to the mosque would be appropriate for mourners. Funerals begin at the mosque, with prayers, before the body is taken to the cemetery (if the mosque has no facilities on site) where final prayers are recited. Burial procedures for all Muslims are the same, as everyone is equal in death : graves are plain, and donations of flowers, for example, would not be appropriate.

Relatives of the deceased are not expected to cook for themselves for forty days after the death, and food provided by relatives, friends and neighbours is appreciated throughout the time of mourning. During this time, family members read the 'Qur'an' all the way through as a gift to the deceased. After the period of mourning, it is customary for the family to provide a meal for relatives and friends at which, traditionally, some of the favourite foods of the deceased are provided in their memory.

Medical Matters

Family planning : Although individual practice may vary, birth control would generally be considered in religious terms as an endeavour to circumvent the will of Allah.

Illness : Visits from the imam are usual for those who are sick, for recitation of special portions of the 'Qu'ran'.

Hospital stays : In medical situations, Muslim men and women would prefer to be treated by medical staff of the same sex, and not to attend for tests in short gowns. Examinations in front of a number of doctors and students would be objectionable as public nakedness is not acceptable to a Muslim. In cases of a longer hospital stay, the use of a shower is preferred to a bath and a container of water for washing purposes should be provided whenever the toilet area is separate from the bathroom. Organ donation, transplants and blood transfusions are not usual, although not forbidden. It is worthy of note that Muslims would not usually expect to have medical information discussed directly with the patient, preferring to refer the matter to second-degree male relatives e.g. uncles and cousins.

If a patient is terminally ill, it would be appreciated if the bed could be turned to face Makkah and if the pillows could be raised so that the patient's head is a little above the rest of the body. Prayers would normally be recited by relatives, friends or the imam.

In the case of death : After death only Muslims should handle the body. Next of kin or the local Muslim community will make arrangements to prepare the body for burial. Autopsies are acceptable only where necessary for the issue of a death certificate or for coronial purposes.

Core belief

To enable the soul at death to reunite with God - of whom it is part - and to achieve this by remembering God constantly in daily life and by truthful living, with service to others being particularly important.

'Rules' of life

A Sikh initiated into the 'Khalsa Panth' believes in the oneness of God, the teachings of the Gurus and the Sikh Scriptures, and always wears the five articles of faith that distinguish Sikhs (see *Dress*).

In practice, remembering God in everyday life through earning a living by ethical means, sharing with the needy and spending time regularly in service to others are all seminal tenets of the Sikh faith.

Holy books

It is important to note that the Sikh Scriptures are treated by Sikhs with the utmost reverence and respect. The original version was compiled by the fifth Guru, Arjan Dev, and contained the teachings of the first five Gurus as well as specifically chosen verses from Hindu and Muslim saintly literature. The hymns of Guru Tegh Bahadur were added by Guru Gobind Singh at a later date to complete the scriptures, known as 'Guru Granth Sahib'.

In addition, Sikhs may refer to the writings of Guru Gobind Singh ('Dasam Granth') and the Sikh Code of Conduct ('Rahit Maryada').

Daily acts of faith

A devout Sikh will rise early, bathe and then spend some time in meditation before saying the morning set prayers, whilst evening prayers are said before sleep. These prayers may be said privately, or with the family. Collective worship is usual on Sundays.

Major annual events

Guru Nanak's Birthday - a three day celebration of the birth of the founder of the Sikh faith.

The Martyrdom of Guru Tegh Bahadur - a commemoration of the death of the Guru executed for his belief in the need for religious liberty and freedom of worship.

Guru Gobind Singh's Birthday - to celebrate the birth of the Guru who instituted the Sikh initiation ceremony and code of discipline.

The Martyrdom of Guru Arjan Dev - in commemoration of the Guru who completed work on the Golden Temple at Amritsar.

Other important festivals include:

Baisakhi - the anniversay of the day when Guru Gobind Singh founded the order of the Khalsa, a time when the Sikh flag which flies outside the Gurdwara is replaced with a new one.

Divali - when Gurdwaras are lit in remembrance of the spiritual victory of Guru Hargobind who delivered fifty-two Hindu kings from imprisonment.

Births

The birth of a baby is a very joyous occasion, with visits to the mother and child taking place as soon as possible, although the mother herself is expected to rest for forty days in order to avoid illness. Gifts of money or clothes for the baby from friends and relatives are traditional, whilst the parents of the child will often distribute sweets in celebration of the event.

As soon as possible after the child's birth, a member of the family will recite a prayer quietly into the baby's ear, but the name of the baby is not known until a few weeks later when the child is welcomed into the wider community of Sikhs at a naming ceremony at the Gurdwara. Prayers are said by the family, the child's name is chosen (to begin with the same first letter as a word chosen at random from the 'Guru Granth Sahib') and the baby is given a little 'amrit', special sweet water.

Names

Sikhs generally have three names : their given name, a title (Singh -"Prince" for all males, Kaur -"Princess" for all females), and finally a family name.

Where names are required for records, the family name can tactfully be asked for, bearing in mind that Sikhs generally prefer to use and will therefore usually offer their first name alone, or their first name together with their title (Singh or Kaur).

Diet

General : Dietary practice varies, but in general Sikhs would not use alcohol, tobacco or drugs, and would refrain from eating beef, pork or halal meat. Many Sikhs are vegetarian and will not eat eggs, nor anything that is produced from animals (such as cheese made with rennet). Salads, rice, dahl, vegetables and fruit are generally acceptable foods to offer.

Specific : Some Sikhs may prefer to fast at the time of a full moon.

Language

Members of Sikh families in the UK may speak several languages other than English, in the main, Punjabi (or Panjabi) and sometimes Swahili. Urdu and Hindi may also be understood to some extent by Panjabi speakers.

The Sikh Scriptures themselves are written in 'Gurmukhi', in which script modern Panjabi is still written. The Panjabi language is therefore held in great esteem in the Sikh communities and classes in it are customarily offered by Gurdwaras.

Dress

To check dress requirements for particular occasions, see the appropriate entry e.g. Marriages.

In general, covering the body is a requirement : tact in discussing joining in with activities such as swimming, and in providing individual changing areas for sports would therefore be appreciated. In addition, all initiated Sikhs, male and female, wear the five 'K' symbols as a sign of their initiation into the Sikh community. These are : Kesh (uncut hair, generally covered with a turban), Kangha (a comb to keep the hair neat), Kara (a steel bangle which symbolises the unity of God), Kirpan (a short dagger which symbolises the readiness of the Sikh to fight against injustice and to protect the oppressed), Kachha (shorts to symbolise modesty). It is important to remember that removal of the Kachha or the turban is a cause of immense embarrassment for a Sikh and should be avoided at all costs.

Visits

Places of worship : A Sikh Gurdwara is generally a centre for educational, social and welfare activities as well as the place for communal worship.

Inside the Gurdwara, the Sikh Scriptures are kept on a covered, low canopy. Offerings of food (fruit, milk or sugar) or money are customarily taken to the Gurdwara to be presented on arrival and, whilst visitors are not expected to make offerings, these will be welcome if proffered.

Clothing for visitors, women and men, should be modest, with long skirts or loose trousers being worn. Covering the head throughout the ceremony is essential for everyone, shoes should be removed before entering the Gurdwara and visitors may be invited to wash their hands, as Sikhs customarily do before prayer. It should also be remembered that it is not permitted to take alcohol, drugs or tobacco into any part of the Gurdwara, so visitors who smoke are asked to leave their cigarettes outside the building.

Upon entering, visitors are invited to show respect to the 'Guru Granth Sahib' by bowing or by standing before it for a few moments in silence and, if offerings have been brought, these can be placed on the floor in front of the Scriptures.

Seating is on the floor, with men and women often sitting in separate groups. It is usual to sit with legs crossed or to the side : pointing the feet towards the 'Guru Granth Sahib', or turning the back towards it are both considered to be disrespectful.

At the end of worship, 'karah prashad' (blessed food) is distributed to all equally, and it would generally be anticipated that visitors receive some. Similarly, visitors would be expected to partake in the 'langar' or communal meal served at the end of worship. As this food is also blessed, head coverings should be maintained, and all food asked for should be eaten rather than left.

Home visiting : Some Sikh homes may contain a copy of the 'Guru Granth Sahib', which is generally kept in a separate room and respect towards this when visiting is appropriate.

Preparation before mealtimes entails washing the hands. At the meal itself, the food is blessed before it is eaten, and food is traditionally taken with the right hand only. After the meal it is customary to give thanks and to wash the hands again. The offering of hospitality is central to Sikh life, so being a considerate guest involves a willingness to reciprocate by sharing in the food and drink offered.

Marriages

A Sikh wedding is a sacred ceremony, that takes place in front of the Sikh Scriptures, when the bride and groom agree to be loyal and kind to each other and their families, in joy and in sorrow. The marriage can be celebrated in a Gurdwara, hall or the bride's home, but as it takes place in front of the Scriptures, dress etiquette for guests should take into account guidelines for visiting a Gurdwara. The bride herself usually wears red or deep pink.

Wedding cards are generally welcome but, in choosing a card, it would be appropriate to remember that many Sikh weddings are 'arranged', so that close members of the family have been involved in the choice of a life partner for the bride and groom. Traditional wedding gifts take the form of money which is taken to the wedding reception and given to the couple by pinning it to the groom's shirt. It is also customary to take rose petals to the wedding, to throw over bride and groom after they are married.

The wedding may be presided over by any Sikh adult well thought of in the community. After a short talk, bride and groom hold either end of the groom's scarf and walk four times around the Scriptures while the Sikh wedding hymn is recited and sung. After the fourth time, the couple are married, and 'karah prashad' is shared amongst everyone present to conclude the ceremony.

After the wedding, there is general feasting for the couple, their relatives and guests, before the bride changes into new clothes and the couple leave for the groom's home to begin their new life.

Funerals

Sikhs are not generally fearful of death, believing that it is possible, by the way in which they live their lives, to escape the cycle of death and rebirth and be reunited with God.

White is customarily worn by mourners, and Sikhs are usually cremated, as soon as possible after death.

The funeral begins at the home of the deceased, where relatives and friends visit to pay their respects, traditionally taking gifts of money, before the coffin is taken to the Gurdwara for prayers. This is followed by a service at the crematorium where there is a reading from the 'Guru Granth Sahib', followed by the evening prayer. Committal of the body is usually undertaken by the eldest son. Mourners then return to the Gurdwara for further prayers, followed by the sharing of 'karah prashad' and a communal meal.

After the funeral, the adults of the family of the deceased share in reading the whole of the 'Guru Granth Sahib', which may take up to two weeks, and this is a time for friends and family to visit in order to offer their sympathy.

Medical Matters

Family planning : There are usually no religious objections to family planning.

Illness : In general, home remedies may be preferred in the first instance, and reading passages from the Scriptures will be of comfort to those who are ill.

Hospital stays : In medical circumstances, most Sikh women would prefer to be examined by a female member of the medical staff, and would not wish to be sent for relevant tests in a short gown. In cases of a longer hospital stay, showers are considered to be preferable to baths, and a container of water for washing purposes should always be provided whenever the toilet area is separate from a bathroom. There are no religious objections to blood transfusions and transplants.

It is important to remember, during medical treatment, that respect should be observed for a Sikh's desire to have all five symbols of the faith within reach if, for some reason, it is not possible for them to be worn, and that Kachha (shorts) should on no account be changed or removed other than by the individual concerned.

In the case of death : After death, the body of the deceased may be handled by non-Sikhs, but it is essential to make sure that the five Sikh symbols are in place. There are no religious objections to autopsies, if absolutely required.

Useful Further Reading

General

All in Good Faith : A Resource Book for Multi-faith Prayer, ed. Jean Potter & Marcus Braybrooke, The World Congress of Faiths, 1997
Eyewitness Guide to Religion, Myrtle Langley, Dorling Kindersley Ltd., 1996
Faith Commandments, The Festival Shop, 1998
My Christian Faith, A. Seaman & A. Brown, Evans Brothers Ltd.,1999
My Hindu Faith, Anita Ganeri, Evans Brothers Ltd., 1999
My Jewish Faith, Anne Clark, Evans Brothers Ltd., 1999
My Muslim Faith, Khadijah Knight, Evans Brothers Ltd., 1999
My Buddhist Life, Meg St. Pierre & Marty Casey, Wayland Publishers Ltd., 1996
My Christian Life, Alison Seaman, Wayland Publishers Ltd., 1996
My Hindu Life, D. Kadodwala & S. Chhapi, Wayland Publishers Ltd., 1996
My Jewish Life, Anne Clark & David Rose, Wayland Publishers Ltd., 1996
My Muslim Life, Riadh El-Droubie, Wayland Publishers Ltd., 1996
My Sikh Life, Kanwaljit Kaur-Singh, Wayland Publishers Ltd., 1996
Religions in the UK : A Multi-Faith Directory, ed. Paul Weller, University of Derby, 1997
Religions of the World, ed. E.Breuilly, J.O'Brien, M.Palmer, Macdonald Young Books, 1997
The Elements of World Religions, Liz Flower, Element Books Ltd., 1997
What do we know about Buddhism?, Anita Ganeri, Macdonald Young Books, 1996
What do we know about Christianity?, Carol Watson, Macdonald Young Books, 1996
What do we know about Hinduism?, Anita Ganeri, Macdonald Young Books, 1996
What do we know about Islam?, Shahrukh Husain, Macdonald Young Books, 1996
What do we know about Judaism?, Doreen Fine, Macdonald Young Books, 1996
What do we know about Sikhism?, Beryl Dhanjal, Macdonald Young Books, 1996
World Religions, John Bowker, Dorling Kindersley Ltd., 1997
World Religions : Buddhism, Catherine Hewitt, Wayland Publishers Ltd., 1995
World Religions : Christianity, John Logan, Wayland Publishers Ltd., 1995
World Religions : Hinduism, Dilip Kadodwala, Wayland Publishers Ltd., 1995
World Religions : Judaism, Angela Wood, Wayland Publishers Ltd., 1995
World Religions : Islam, Khadijah Knight, Wayland Publishers Ltd., 1995
World Religions : Sikhism, Kanwaljit Kaur-Singh, Wayland Publishers Ltd., 1995

Life Events

New Beginnings (Celebrating Birth), Anita Ganeri, Evans Brothers Ltd., 1998
Growing Up (From Child to Adult), Anita Ganeri, Evans Brothers Ltd., 1998
Wedding Days (Celebrations of Marriage), Anita Ganeri, Evans Brothers Ltd., 1998
Journey's End (Death & Mourning), Anita Ganeri, Evans Brothers Ltd., 1998

Places of Worship

Buddhist Vihara, Anita Ganeri, A. & C. Black (Publishers) Ltd., 1998
Christian Church, Alan Brown & Alison Seaman, A. & C. Black (Publishers) Ltd., 1998
Hindu Mandir, Anita Ganeri, A. & C Black (Publishers) Ltd., 1998
Jewish Synagogue, Laurie Rosenberg, A. & C. Black (Publishers) Ltd., 1998
Muslim Mosque, Umar Hegedus, A. & C. Black (Publishers) Ltd., 1998
Sikh Gurdwara, Kanwaljit Kaur-Singh, A. & C. Black (Publishers), 1998

Index

Index

NOTES

To the very best of our knowledge, all the information that we provide fairly represents the faiths and is accurate. Please do remember, though, that there is always room for interpretation, especially given the wide range of orthodoxy that exists in any faith, and it is therefore advisable to liaise directly with your own local faith communities around particular events.

Note on vegetarianism

Vegetarianism means many things to many people but, in general, removing meat foods from a plate will not render the rest of the meal acceptable and composite menu items e.g. 'Scotch broth' may be difficult for a vegetarian to evaluate. Having a clearly labelled vegetarian option (ie without meat, fish, dairy products or eggs) available on every menu would be ideal.